LYNX VS. PORCUPINES

FOOD CHAIN FIGHTS

BEN HUBBARD

Lerner Publications ◆ Minneapolis

For the girls: Krysia, Magda, and Zosia

Lerner Publications Company
An imprint of Lerner Publishing Group, Inc.
241 First Avenue North
Minneapolis, MN 55401 USA

For reading levels and more information, look up this title at www.lernerbooks.com.

Main body text set in Aptifer Sans LT Pro.
Typeface provided by Linotype AG.

Editor: Nicole Berglund **Photo Editor:** Nicole Berglund

Library of Congress Cataloging-in-Publication Data

Names: Hubbard, Ben, 1973– author.
Title: Lynx vs. porcupines : food chain fights / Ben Hubbard.
Other titles: Lynx versus porcupines
Description: Minneapolis : Lerner Publications , [2025] | Series: Predator vs. prey | Includes bibliographical references and index. | Audience: Ages 8–11 | Audience: Grades 4–6 | Summary: "The Canadian lynx is known for camouflage and hunting. But the porcupine's sharp quills are an excellent defense. Readers will learn important features of each animal and discover who rules the North American forests"— Provided by publisher.
Identifiers: LCCN 2024013841 (print) | LCCN 2024013842 (ebook) | ISBN 9798765647325 (library binding) | ISBN 9798765662168 (paperback) | ISBN 9798765657034 (epub)
Subjects: LCSH: Lynx—Juvenile literature. | Porcupines—Juvenile literature. | Animal defenses—Juvenile literature. | Predation (Biology)—Juvenile literature.
Classification: LCC QL737.C23 H833 2025 (print) | LCC QL737.C23 (ebook) | DDC 599.35/97—dc23/eng/20240620

LC record available at https://lccn.loc.gov/2024013841
LC ebook record available at https://lccn.loc.gov/2024013842

Manufactured in the United States of America
1-1010995-53172-7/15/2024

TABLE OF CONTENTS

CHAPTER 1

MEET THE ANIMALS

IT IS DAWN IN A DENSE FIR FOREST. It is slowly becoming light. A North American porcupine walks past a hollow log. But it is being watched. Inside the log is a Canada lynx. The lynx has been waiting all night for a meal. Now it has a chance to ambush the porcupine.

The lynx wriggles out of the log and pounces. It bats the porcupine with its large paw. The blow knocks the porcupine onto its back. The porcupine is stunned and stays still. Its soft belly is exposed. Now the lynx can have its meal. But the lynx yelps in pain. Its paw is full of sharp porcupine quills.

The North American porcupine is among the largest rodents in the world!

Canada lynx and porcupines share forests across North America. The lynx is a predator that is rarely seen. It is good at hiding. It can stay still, hidden for hours behind fallen trees, broken branches, and in hollow logs. The lynx then launches surprise attacks on prey such as snowshoe hares, birds, and porcupines.

The Canada lynx is nocturnal, meaning it is mostly awake at night.

CANADA LYNX STATS

WEIGHT: 20 to 40 pounds (9 to 18 kg)

LENGTH: 30 to 42 inches (76 to 107 cm)

TOP SPEED: 30 miles (48 km) per hour

PORCUPINE STATS

WEIGHT: 15 to 27 pounds (7 to 12 kg)

LENGTH: 25 to 36 inches (64 to 91 cm)

TOP SPEED: 2 miles (3.2 km) per hour

The porcupine is a small, slow herbivore. It eats berries, leaves, and tree bark. It is prey for predators such as foxes, fishers, and Canada lynx. But the porcupine does not hide like the lynx. This is because it is one of the best-protected animals in the forest. It is covered with long, sharp spines called quills. This makes it hard to eat!

Canada lynx and porcupines are both armed for battle. But which would win in a fight? Let's find out!

In the winter, North American porcupines mostly eat evergreen needles and tree bark.

The Canada lynx's giant paws allow the lynx to easily walk on snow.

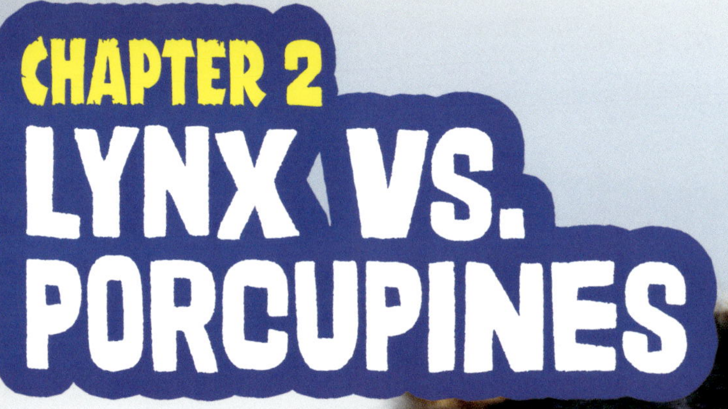

CHAPTER 2
LYNX VS. PORCUPINES

CANADA LYNX AND PORCUPINES HAVE SPECIAL TRAITS TO HELP THEM STAY ALIVE. These include size, strength, and senses. Let's compare their features to choose a ruler of the forest habitat.

Different species of
lynx are found across
North America, Europe,
and Asia.

FLUFFY FUR

Canada lynx have two layers of fur to stay warm in winter. One layer is fluffy, and the other layer is thick and long.

SIZE

The Canada lynx has a short body, long legs, and padded paws. It looks like a big house cat with a short tail and tufts of black fur on its ears. In winter, the lynx has long, gray fur. In summer, the fur is short and light brown. This ensures the Canada lynx has year-round camouflage.

The porcupine is small with stocky legs. It has a club-shaped tail. It is covered with soft brown-and-gray hair, and about thirty thousand sharp quills. Porcupines have round heads, tiny ears, and black eyes. They also have long claws on their feet.

A Canada lynx jumps over a log.

STRENGTH

The Canada lynx has long, strong back legs to help it leap. The lynx can leap a distance of 25 feet (7.6 m). This lets it pounce on prey and jump between trees. The lynx also has big, broad paws. These help the lynx walk across snow without sinking down.

The porcupine is small but strong. It has muscular legs and a powerful tail. It uses its tail to defend itself and to climb trees. The tail helps the porcupine balance on branches. When it is on the ground, a porcupine looks like a round, armored ball.

PORCUPINE DENS

Porcupines make their dens in hollow logs and caves. They poop at the den's entrance. This marks their territory.

North American porcupines' hollow quills allow them to float in water so they can swim!

SENSES

The Canada lynx has strong senses to hunt with. It has large eyes to see at night. It can see prey 250 feet (76 m) away in the dark. It also has excellent hearing. The lynx's large, triangle-shaped ears help it hear approaching prey while it waits to ambush.

The porcupine has amazing senses of hearing and smell. It depends on its ears and nose to detect predators. This is because its eyesight is poor. A porcupine may sense a predator is near but not be able to see it.

LYNX LITTERS

Canada lynx females are pregnant for about sixty days. They give birth to about three kittens. The kittens leave their mothers after one year.

Canada lynx can live about twenty years.

AGILITY

The Canada lynx is an agile creature built to kill. The lynx uses its long legs to jump high and pounce on prey. It can also make several leaps through deep snow. The lynx is an excellent tree climber. Long claws on its paws let the lynx bound up tree trunks.

NIGHT LIVING

Porcupines mostly come out at night. During the day, they sleep in trees or among plants on the ground. The Canada lynx also mostly hunts at night.

The porcupine looks slow and clumsy on land. But like the lynx, it is at home in trees. The porcupine climbs a tree by digging into the bark with its curved claws. It pushes upward with the leathery skin on its feet. Porcupines often spend most of the day in a tree. They climb down tailfirst. Sometimes they miss their step and fall! This can injure the porcupine.

North American porcupines can live up to eighteen years.

Canada lynx have twenty-eight sharp teeth, including four long canines at the front of their mouths.

WARNING SOUNDS

The Canada lynx makes a series of warning sounds when it is threatened. These include yelps, grunts, and barks. It also makes a long, low growl. But its loudest warning is a high-pitched screech. It makes this screech when under attack by a predator, such as a wolf, or when challenged by another lynx.

SNACKING ON SNOWSHOES

The snowshoe hare is the Canada lynx's main prey. The lynx eats around two hundred hares every year.

The porcupine also has several warning sounds. It clacks its teeth. It grunts, groans, shrieks, and barks. It also slaps its tail on the ground. If this does not warn a predator away, the porcupine produces a stinky odor from its skin.

Porcupines chew on bones to get minerals and to grind down their teeth so they don't get too long!

KEY WEAPONS

The Canada lynx is armed with sharp claws and long canine teeth. To attack its prey, the lynx pounces and holds the prey down with its paws. It then gives the prey a fatal bite to its neck.

A porcupine's key weapons are its quills. The quills are like sharp, hollow needles. They attach themselves to any animal that touches the porcupine. The quills are covered in barbs. This means they are hard to remove. Porcupines grow new quills to replace the ones they lose.

QUILL THROWING?

It is often thought that porcupines can throw their quills. But this is not correct. Instead, the quills simply come out easily when touched.

A Canada lynx blends into rocks.

SCAVENGE TO SURVIVE

Canada lynx do not usually attack large prey, such as deer. But they scavenge on the flesh of dead animals.

ATTACK AND DEFENSE STYLES

The Canada lynx is an ambush hunter. It finds a hiding place near prey trails. It then sits and waits. Sometimes it waits for hours. When its prey walks past, the lynx jumps on it. It can also run fast for short distances to catch prey.

When under attack, a porcupine raises its quills. It sometimes spins around in a circle. It then keeps its back to its attacker. If the predator comes close, the porcupine takes a swipe with its tail. This stuns a predator and fills it with quills. Predators often stop their attack afterward.

A Canada lynx rests in grass.

WEAKNESSES

The Canada lynx cannot run fast for long distances. It escapes predators such as wolves by climbing a tree. But it has little chance if caught in the open. So the lynx needs to stay under the cover of trees.

GRINDING TEETH

Porcupines are rodents. This means their teeth never stop growing. They have to grind down their teeth on things such as tree bark and branches.

The porcupine has weak eyesight. It often cannot see where a predator is. The porcupine's other weak parts are its face and stomach. It does not grow quills in these places. Predators successfully hunt the porcupine by flipping it onto its back or biting its face.

Porcupine quills can be hard to see underneath the soft hairs that grow between them, but the quills can be raised at any time.

CHAPTER 3 THE WINNER

THE CANADA LYNX BITES AT THE QUILLS STUCK IN ITS PAW. This gives the porcupine time to roll onto its feet. It lets off a strong smell and screeches loudly. It then runs to a nearby tree and starts to climb.

Meanwhile, the lynx has pulled the quills from its paw. It has not finished its attack. It leaps onto the tree and starts to climb after the porcupine. But it stops below the porcupine. Its claws dig into the tree trunk. It watches and waits for a chance to attack the porcupine's face or stomach.

A porcupine uses its tough, hairless hands to grip onto a tree branch.

The porcupine walks onto a long branch. But the lynx is right behind it. It stretches out a paw and tries to knock the porcupine off. The porcupine swings its tail at the lynx. It hits it in the face. The lynx's soft face now has quills sticking out. It yelps and quickly climbs down the tree. The attack is over.

A Canada lynx stalks prey.

Baby porcupines are called porcupettes.

RULER OF THE HABITAT

The Canada lynx is one of the most successful predators in the forest. But today it has met its match. The porcupine is not large or fast. But it is well protected. It can often fight off an attacker with its long, sharp quills. On another day, the lynx could beat the porcupine and claim its prize. This is the story of survival in the never-ending battle between predator and prey.

PREDATOR VS. PREY: HEAD-TO-HEAD

CANADA LYNX

- Broad, padded paws for walking across snow
- Long, powerful legs for leaping at prey

PORCUPINE

- Around thirty thousand long, sharp quills
- Powerful, club-shaped tail for swiping at predators

GLOSSARY

agile: able to move quickly and easily

ambush: a surprise attack made from a hiding place

camouflage: colors or markings that help animals blend into their surroundings

fatal: ending in death

flesh: the substance between an animal's skin and bone

habitat: the home of an animal or plant

herbivore: an animal that only eats plants, not meat

predator: an animal that hunts and kills other animals for food

prey: an animal that is hunted and killed for food by a predator

sense: the ways an animal understands its surroundings. The five senses are touch, smell, taste, sight, and hearing.

stun: to cause someone or something to suddenly become very confused

LEARN MORE

Britannica Kids: Lynx
https://kids.britannica.com/kids/article/lynx/353403

Britannica Kids: Porcupine
https://kids.britannica.com/kids/article/porcupine/353658

Geister-Jones, Sophie. *Lynx*. Mendota Heights, MN: Apex, 2022.

Kissock, Heather. *Porcupine*. New York: Lightbox Learning, 2022.

National Geographic Kids: Porcupine
https://kids.nationalgeographic.com/animals/mammals/facts/porcupine

Roggio, Sarah. *Tigers vs. Deer: Food Chain Fights*. Minneapolis: Lerner Publications, 2025.

INDEX

PHOTO ACKNOWLEDGMENTS

Image credits: jared lloyd/Getty Images, pp. 4–5; Holly Kuchera/Shutterstock, p. 6; mlorenzphotography/Getty Images, pp. 7 (top), 28; Richard Wear/Getty Images, p. 7 (bottom); rixonline/Getty Images, p. 8; Cavan Images/Getty Images, p. 9; jimkruger/Getty Images, pp. 10–11; Christina Radcliffe/Getty Images, pp. 12, 17; Kathleen Reeder Wildlife Photography/Getty Images, pp. 13, 15, 23; Dopeyden/Getty Images, p. 14; Carol Gray/Shutterstock, p. 16; Holly Kuchera/Alamy, p. 18; Sandra Mitchell/Getty Images, p. 19; Gerald Corsi/Getty Images, p. 20; Malcolm Schuyl/Alamy, p. 21; Mark Newman/Getty Images, p. 22; Scott Shymko/Getty Images, pp. 24–25; slowmotiongli/Getty Images, p. 26; Sabih Jafri/Getty Images, p. 27; Joel Bailey/500px/Getty Images, p. 29. Design elements: iunewind/Shutterstock; Milano M/Shutterstock; Cassel/Shutterstock; Textures and backgrounds/Shutterstock; Print Net/Shutterstock; Ukrainian studio/Shutterstock.

Cover: Ibrahim Suha Derbent/Getty Images; Rita Petcu/Shutterstock.